Pe

The

MW01146695

The Story of Peter
Accurately retold from the Bible
(from the book of Acts)
by Carine Mackenzie

Illustrations by
Duncan McLaren
Cover design by Daniel van Straaten

© Copyright 1988 Christian Focus Publications
ISBN 978-1-84550-170-9

Reprinted 1992, 1998, 2000, 2006, 2009 and 2014

Published in Great Britain by
Christian Focus Publications
Geanies House, Fearn, Tain, Ross-shire, IV20 1TW, Scotland.
www.christianfocus.com

Printed in China

Peter was a close friend of Jesus. Shortly before Jesus returned to heaven, he spoke specially to Peter asking him to 'feed his lambs.' He wanted Peter to preach the gospel to everyone. Peter spent the rest of his life telling others the good news about Jesus.

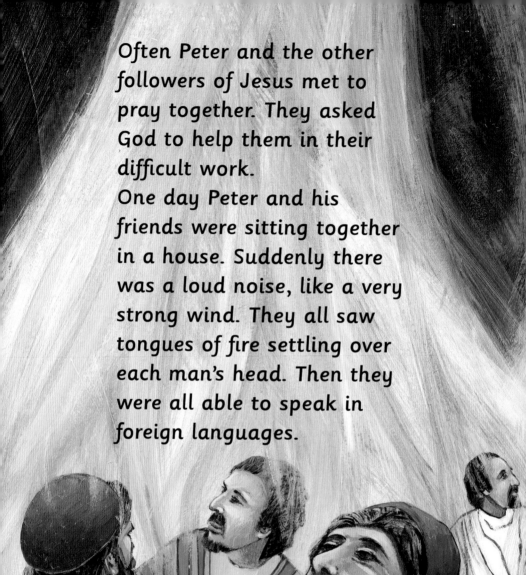

Often Peter and the other followers of Jesus met to pray together. They asked God to help them in their difficult work.

One day Peter and his friends were sitting together in a house. Suddenly there was a loud noise, like a very strong wind. They all saw tongues of fire settling over each man's head. Then they were all able to speak in foreign languages.

How amazing! How could this happen? God, the Holy Spirit, had come and had given his power to each man, to help him in the work of preaching the gospel. These men became known as apostles.

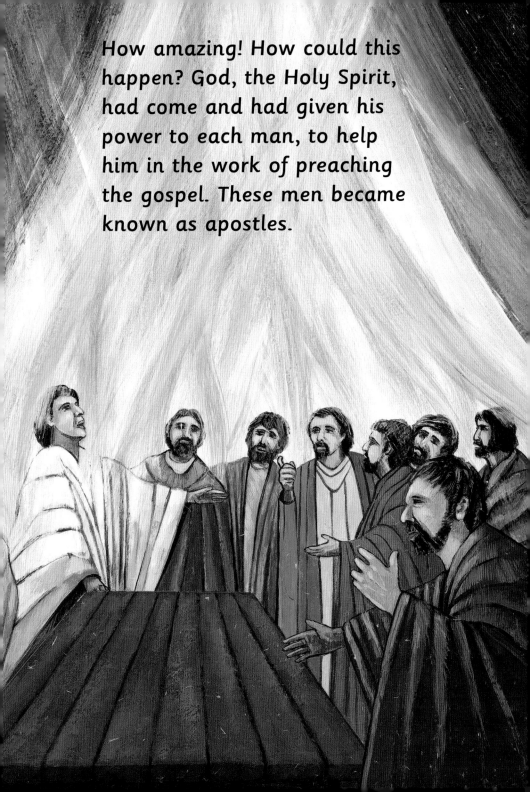

Many foreign visitors were in Jerusalem at that time. When they heard that Peter and the other Galilean men were speaking in foreign languages they were amazed and came to hear them for themselves. They all heard the message of the gospel in their own languages. Many were astonished by the power of God but some laughed and said, 'Oh they must be drunk'.

Peter stood up and spoke to the crowd. 'Listen to me,' he said. 'These men are not drunk. It is only nine o'clock in the morning. The Holy Spirit has come to these men. Let me tell you about Jesus. Remember, he did many wonderful miracles, you took him and cruelly killed him, but he rose from the dead.'

The people listening asked Peter and the others, 'What must we do?' Peter told them, 'Repent and be baptized every one of you in the name of Jesus Christ.' On that day about 3,000 people believed and put their trust in Jesus.

We need to be truly sorry for our sins and ask Jesus to forgive us.

One afternoon, Peter and John went together to the temple to pray. At the gate, called the Beautiful Gate, sat a lame man. He had been disabled from birth. Every day he was carried to the gate so that he could sit and beg from the people passing by.

When he saw Peter and John he asked them for some money. They stopped and stared at the man. 'Look at us,' said Peter. 'I have no silver or gold, but I will give you something else. In the name of Jesus Christ of Nazareth rise up and walk.' He took him by the right hand and pulled him to his feet.

Immediately he felt strength surging into his feet and ankles. He was able to walk for the first time ever. He went into the temple with Peter and John jumping for joy and praising God.

The people recognised him and could hardly believe that the man walking into the temple was the same man who used to sit begging at the Beautiful Gate.

God loves to hear praise. He wants to hear you praise him and thank him for all his goodness to you.

Peter preached to the crowd in the temple urging them to repent of their sins and to trust in Jesus as their Saviour. But the religious leaders had Peter and John thrown into prison.

The next day these leaders and officials questioned Peter and John. Peter told them that all they did was through the power of Jesus. The leaders were surprised at how well Peter spoke. They realised that he had been with Jesus.

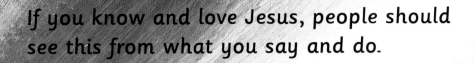

If you know and love Jesus, people should see this from what you say and do.

The Christians showed great love to each other and cared for each other. They shared all their possessions. Those who had money gave it freely, those who had land sold it to raise money. Some even sold their houses.

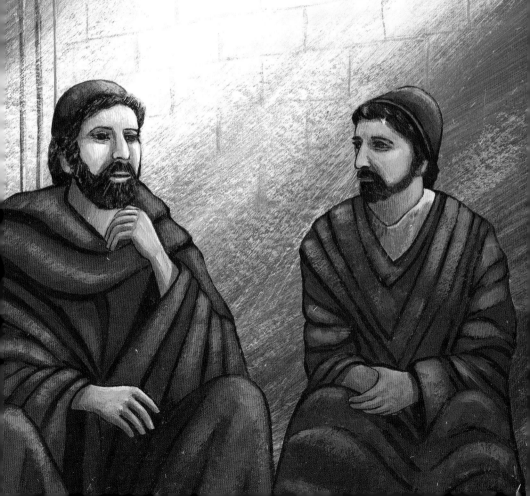

One couple called Ananias and Sapphira decided to sell their land. Ananias took the money to Peter. 'Here's all the money we got for our land,' he said. But he was lying. They had kept some of the money for themselves. Peter knew that he was not telling the truth. Peter said to Ananias, 'The land was yours. The money you received was yours. Why did you pretend that you had given ALL the money? You have lied to God.' When Ananias heard these words, he fell down dead.

Everyone who heard Peter's words, was very shocked at what happened. The young men carried his body out of the house and buried him.

About three hours later Sapphira returned, not knowing what had happened to her husband. Peter said to her, 'Did you really sell the land for so much?' 'Oh yes,' she said. 'That was the price.' 'Oh, you have agreed together to cheat God, the Holy Spirit. The men who have just buried your husband are at the door. They will carry your body out to be buried too.' She immediately dropped down dead. Everyone who knew her was very shocked.

It is very wrong to tell a lie, no matter what the situation. God is angry with the sin of lying. He wants us to tell the truth, always.

Peter and the apostles did many wonderful miracles, healing sick people. The people were amazed and many believed in the Lord Jesus. But the Jewish leaders were very angry and again they threw Peter into prison.

That night an angel of the Lord opened the prison doors. So Peter and the others went back to the temple to teach the people about Jesus.
The High Priest was even more angry, but Peter said, 'We ought to obey God rather than men.'

In the end the apostles were beaten but allowed to go free. They were happy that they were worthy to suffer for the sake of Jesus.

Peter travelled round the country telling people the good news of the gospel. One day he came to a place called Lydda. There he met a man who had been in bed for eight years, unable to walk. Peter said to him, 'Aeneas, Jesus Christ makes you whole, get up and make your bed.' He immediately rose up. Many people who saw the wonderful happening came to believe on the Lord.

In the next town of Joppa, lived a lady called Dorcas. She was a follower of the Lord Jesus and spent her time helping others. She made coats and dresses for the local poor children and their mothers. One day Dorcas fell ill and died. Her friends were very upset.

What would they do without Dorcas?
'Have you heard what happened at
Lydda?' someone said. 'Peter cured that
man, Aeneas. He can walk now. He spoke
to him the name of Jesus.'

'Someone should go to Lydda and fetch
Peter. He may do something for Dorcas.'

As soon as Peter was asked he went with the men to Dorcas' house. Dorcas' friends were weeping in her room. They showed Peter the clothes that Dorcas had made for them.

Peter told them all to leave the room. He kneeled down and prayed – then turned to Dorcas and said, 'Get up.' She opened her eyes and when she saw Peter, she sat up. Peter took her hand and helped her out of bed. He called all her friends back – 'Here is Dorcas, well again.'

News of this wonderful happening spread through Joppa and many believed in the Lord Jesus as a result.

Herod, the king, hated the Christian church. He was very cruel to them — even killing some. He took Peter and had him thrown in prison. The Christian friends were very concerned for him and prayed to God continually for him. One night Peter was sleeping, chained between two soldiers. The prison was locked and guarded.

An angel of the Lord came to the prison and woke Peter. 'Get up quickly,' he said. The chains fell off his hands. 'Get dressed and put on your sandals,' he added 'and follow me.'

Peter did as he was told, but he thought he was dreaming. Could this really be happening?

Past one guard they went, then another, right out into the street. Peter realised then that God had delivered him from prison.

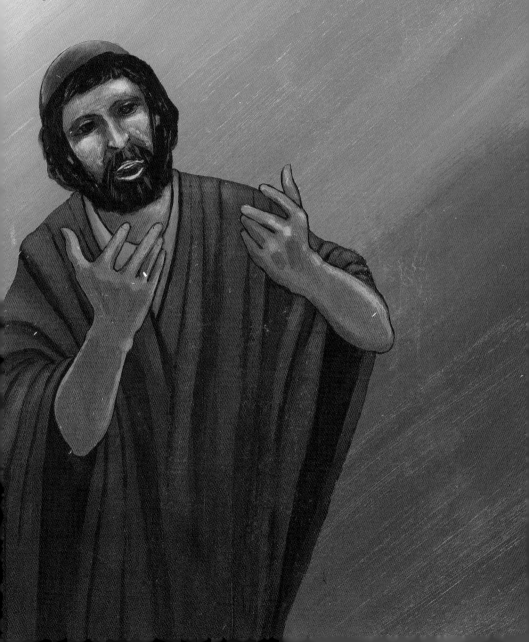

Many Christians had met in Mary's house to pray for Peter.

A knock came on the outside door. A girl called Rhoda ran to the door to answer it. She heard Peter's voice. She was so surprised that she did not open the door, but ran back inside to tell the others. 'Don't talk nonsense,' they said. 'It is Peter,' she insisted. 'I know his voice.'

But Peter kept on knocking and eventually the door was opened and when they saw Peter they were all amazed. He told them how the Lord had brought him out of prison. 'Go and tell my friends the good news.' He then went away to a place where Herod would not find him.

Peter's great work was telling others about Jesus the Saviour. Even when he met with difficulty and opposition he still obeyed Jesus' command. He brought the gospel, not only to the Jewish people, but he believed that the gospel should be preached to people of every nation. Some of the church leaders disagreed with Peter about this, but he explained how God had guided him to preach the gospel to Cornelius, a Roman soldier, and his household and how God had blessed his work. The church leaders were very satisfied and glorified God. They were pleased that God's mercy was offered to people of any nation.
The work of God spread and prospered.